Take Bless Break, Give

Celebrating
throughout the year

Vaughan Jones

ISBN 0 85346 218 6

© The United Reformed Church, 2003

by Vaughan Jones

Published by Granary Press
the imprint of The United Reformed Church
86 Tavistock Place, London WC1H 9RT

Produced by Communications and Editorial, Graphics Office

Printed by mcp goldies limited,
Units B2 & B3, 16-16a Baldwins Gardens,
Hatton Square, London EC1N 7RJ

This book is dedicated to the memory of my father, Revd R Glyn Jones, a Congregationalist Minister with an ecumenical vision.

Poetry is the refuge of those who have not the Catholic Church to flee to and repose upon.

Keble

take, bless, break, give

Contents

Foreword

Out of all that is good in the Reformed tradition, the thing most precious to me is liturgical freedom. I think I might even be prepared to die for it. There is no substitute for the directness and truth of worship in which we speak to God out of the realities of our lives, here and now, and listen for God's word to us in the way that good worship leadership enables us to do. Worship comes alive when ministers and lay preachers use their own words and images to lift people's prayers to God in language that is fresh and immediate. Scripture becomes startlingly relevant as they allow it to speak to today's world.

Ancient prayers have their place too, of course. They remind us of our deep roots and our reliance on the faith of those who went before us. But we claim that faith for ourselves when we articulate it in the language of our generation. Yes, sometimes we make a mess of it! We take risks, and some of them don't work. But when we get it right, you can feel the Holy Spirit of God alive in the Church. I'm talking goose bumps, the hair standing up on the back of your head, the shiver running up your spine. And your spirit enabled to feel and express something that might never have been conscious before.

Vaughan Jones is one of the ministers who get it right. Every one of his prayers has echoes of the East London congregation he serves and the centre for refugees and asylum seekers where he works. The language is quietly but uncompromisingly inclusive. How we need that, if we are to be a truly inclusive Church! He prays for justice in words that reflect the conflicts, tensions and possibilities of the global village in which we live. When he asks the Spirit to come, he is asking that God's power and healing be released in real situations. The prayers ring with the urgency of someone who actually believes in a God who can make a difference.

Vaughan's special gift is to say something fresh and contemporary while still firmly rooted in Christian tradition. It was Vaughan who taught me the story of St. Yared of Ethiopia, remembered as the author of the Orthodox liturgy. Yared was visited by three birds (one green, one yellow, one red – the colours of the Ethiopian flag) who transported him to heaven to hear the angels singing. Overwhelmed and scarcely able to believe his ears, he listened intently. When he had been returned to earth, he transcribed what he had heard; that transcription was the basis for the traditional liturgy of the Church. Perhaps it is the business of all of us who lead earthly saints in their worship, to be aware of a greater song resounding just beyond our senses and to try to give it voice through the humble media of word and sign and music. Vaughan is intentional in setting himself to

3

that task. Some readers will recognise a continuity with the tradition of the Church in Vaughan's work which is lacking in many contemporary worship anthologies. Vaughan's hope is that this combination of deep rootedness in tradition and fresh openness to the present will help to create a new ecumenical meeting ground on which Catholic and Reformed Christians can worship together without either feeling a sense of "second best". I share that hope.

The book is not simply a collection of words. Vaughan encourages us to ring bells, to light candles, to get out of our pews and move in response to the gospel. At this point, we may sense a few Reformed ancestors turning in their graves. Let them turn! It is time to re-engage the senses in worship, to move beyond the cerebral to deeper levels of knowing and praying. Too often newcomers attend our services and fail to find the connection with mystery that they seek. Vaughan's suggestions can help. There are no gimmicks here, only a conviction that true worship is not purely an intellectual exercise.

I hope that these prayers will be widely used in our churches. I hope even more that they will encourage other worship leaders to engage in the demanding but rewarding work of creating their own liturgies. The God who speaks afresh to us in every generation deserves the best we can offer in return.

Roberta Rominger

Introduction
Introduction

Introduction

Sunday by Sunday, season by season, Christians take bread, bless it, break it and share it. It is a simple thing to do. It unites us in our memory of Jesus and the richness of his story. It points us forward to our dream of the new world we desire. It shapes our present commitment to a way of life, in which the resources of the earth and humanity are taken reverently, blessed by God's grace, exposed in their weakness and vulnerability, and then shared equitably and generously.

This collection of Eucharistic prayers and related material was written and re-written over a number of years for use within a local congregation in East London, as we have taken bread, blessed, broken, and shared it.

They are not really new because they are structured within the tradition of the church, which reaches back to the earliest days of the resurrected Christ. The prayer has not changed, only the rhythm and the immediacy of the language. These are dialogue prayers in which the congregation and the President talk to each other and to God. They are a drama, which leads us step by step into the mystery of communion, through which God's grace speaks and the Kingdom of God is opened.

Whilst the main body of these prayers are Eucharistic, we must not forget that the Eucharistic prayer is the culmination of the whole liturgy. They cannot stand alone out of context. For this reason, prayers have been included for use at other parts of the service.

There is a pattern in the prayers, which becomes memorable with regular use. There is variation between the seasons, so that we are freshly challenged and sense the rhythm of time, whilst maintaining familiarity.

They are written in the firm conviction that the Eucharist, whilst it may take us away from our day-to-day struggles for a while, is a vital component if not the essential in building wholeness, integrity, justice and peace in a strife-torn world. We do not have the luxury of choosing between the concrete pastoral work of justice and peace and our spiritual growth. They are one and the same mutually dependent task.

Christians are united in the Eucharist, even though it is a cause of our division. These prayers are a contribution from an independent strand of Christian life – rooted as they are in the enduring Puritan claim to freedom of worship in the Holy Spirit. However, they are also the outcome of an ecumenical journey in modern times and the bold claim that all Christian tradition belongs to all Christians. They resist sectarianism. They take from tradition, ask God to bless it, break it through Christ's love and then share it afresh as Christians. There is an unashamed ecumenical ambition underlying the writing of these prayers. Organic unity of Christ's people may seem a long way off. It is often assumed that Eucharistic sharing is the most difficult obstacle to our ecumenism. Yet in the structure and form of the Eucharist, Christian communions are drawing ever closer to each other. The denomination of which we as a worshipping community are a part – the United Reformed Church – was formed as a risk for unity. In developing a catholic Eucharistic liturgy without abandoning our tradition of freedom of worship, we believe that we continuing the risk-taking which gave birth to our denomination. Perhaps the only true ecumenical journey is backwards to the Upper Room – making the Reformation and its tragic divisions redundant.

Our community is set in a difficult context. Our congregation know the realities of war and violence first hand. Our neighbourhood is a crossroads of the world's problems. It is a meeting place for people of different faiths and cultures. The worship which we develop has to be rooted in the quest for God's justice. We cannot be satisfied with temporary political or social solutions. We crave for something deep rooted and permanent. We need faith – but not a remote faith. We have to have an urgent sense of the coming kingdom. This urgency is at the root of the Eucharist. It is a ritual which makes the Kingdom immediately and concretely present. When we share the peace and share Christ's body and blood together – we break down the divisions which the world has created between us.

When we give one to the other with respect and peace, we open the way to a much richer sharing with the whole inhabited earth, the theatre of God's justice. It is our fervent conviction that the Eucharistic ethic of taking, blessing, breaking and sharing is the ethic which inspires our work for justice. It is the "liturgy after the liturgy" – the service which follows and precedes all our services.

How to use this book

Worship leaders are invited to use this as a resource book. The prayers included here are written for congregational use. Please photocopy them and use them in your church. Permission should be sought to reproduce in other publications.

The book follows the patterns of the seasons. This is the rhythm of God beating throughout creation and history. They tell the story of the liberation and release from the burden of corruption and domination. In the liturgy, therefore, we are moving outside the mono-time of modern culture into another space. This should be reflected in the liturgy. Some of the prayers can be used in ordinary time but others are very specific to the day or season.

They should be used within the shape of the liturgy, in its two parts – the Liturgy of the Word and the Liturgy of the faithful. Some of the prayers are a resource to be used as is appropriate within the Liturgy of the Word and the Eucharistic Prayers are the Liturgy of the Faithful.

The Eucharistic Prayers are written with a flow and awareness of the tradition. It is not a good idea to use sections of them and to cut and paste between them as they will lose the structure and with it their basis in liturgical tradition.

Our spirituality is enhanced by familiarity. It is worth being consistent in using them over a period of time. By using them regularly, the prayers become part of the movement of God's time within the life of the community.

The text has words in bold and plain text. Words in bold are spoken by the whole congregation. Do not be tempted to say all the words yourself. The dialogue enables full participation in the drama of the prayer.

Simple gestures should be used by the President. The gifts of bread and wine should be held up for the congregation to see at the Offertory. Hands should be held over the elements during the epiclesis (the invocation of the Holy Spirit). The cup and plate held up for the doxology (through whom, with whom etc). The bread is broken after the peace as the words of the Fraction are said.

Music is interchangeable. There are other settings of the Kyrie, Sanctus, Agnus Dei, Alleluia and Gloria, which can be substituted. Don't be afraid to experiment. Instruments will also have their own liturgical language. Use Latin American or African drumming to accompany the prayers and attune us to the heartbeat of God. Flutes and harps evoke biblical praise. The trumpet is the instrument, which will announce the Jubilee. Meditation bells or temple gongs from Asia prompt deeper prayer or the sacredness of particular moments. They are may also be used as calls to prayer. The angelus[1] is the traditional Christian call to prayer, evoking the trinity and the annunciation to Mary.

Worship can be enhanced by the use of space, incense, colour, art and music. Words alone are inadequate for the variety of levels through which we need to move in the spiritual process of the liturgy.

Above all create sacred space for the words to speak and the Spirit to enter. The aesthetic of liturgy belongs to culture and time. The liturgy itself belongs to God's time. There is no imperative upon us to be relevant to a corrupted world but an onerous responsibility to perform the rituals which connect the present times to the eternal. We need to be modern and traditional at the same time.

---

1   Three strikes of three followed by nine in succession.

Advent

take, bless, break, give

Advent

Advent candles

Lord have mercy

(full music page 133)

Lord have mercy, Lord have mercy,
Lord have mercy on us all.
Lord have mercy, Lord have mercy,
Lord have mercy on us all.[2]

Advent One   In the dawning
and the ending
there is hope.

Advent Two   In the dawning
and the ending
there is hope.
In the anger
and the conflict
there is prophecy.

Advent Three   In the dawning
and the ending
there is hope.
In the anger
and the conflict
there is prophecy.
In denunciation
and accusation
there is John the Baptister.

2   Israeli Mass

Advent Four

In the dawning
and the ending
there is hope.
In the anger
and the conflict
there is prophecy.
In denunciation
and accusation
there is John the Baptister.
In the annunciation
and the proclamations
there is Mary.

Christ have mercy

Christ, have mer - cy, Christ, have mer - cy, Christ have mer - cy on us all.

Christ, have mer - cy, Christ have mer - cy, Christ, have mer - cy on us all.

(full music page 133)

Christ have mercy, Christ have mercy,
Christ have mercy on us all.
Christ have mercy, Christ have mercy,
Christ have mercy on us all.

Advent One

We light a candle for hope.
In the light, we dream.

Advent Two

We light a candle for hope.
In the light, we dream.
We light a candle for the prophets.
In the light, we defy the shadows.

Advent Three

We light a candle for hope.
In the light, we dream.
We light a candle for the prophets.
In the light, we defy the shadows.
We light a candle for John the Baptist.
In the light, we prepare the way.

Advent Four

We light a candle for hope.
In the light, we dream.
We light a candle for the prophets.
In the light, we defy the shadows.
We light a candle for John the Baptist.
In the light, we prepare the way.
We light a candle for Mary.
In the light, there is birth.

Lord have mercy

(full music page 133)

**Lord have mercy, Lord have mercy,
Lord have mercy on us all.
Lord have mercy, Lord have mercy,
Lord have mercy on us all.**

God of expectation,
Grace us in our waiting.
God of prophecy,
Grace us in our speaking.
God of challenges,
Grace us in our denouncing.
God of Good News,
Grace us in our announcing.
God of birth,
**Grace us with your newness,
fondness, simplicity and joy.
Amen.**

Advent Eucharistic Prayer

These are our gifts of bread and wine.
We bring them to God.

We come to receive the God, who comes.
With open hearts and longing souls.

Blessed be God!
Blessed be God forever!

The Lord be with you!
And also with you!

Lift up your hearts!
We lift them to the Lord!

Let us give thanks to God!
It is right to give God thanks and praise!

We praise you because you care for us and love us.
From the beginning of time to the end of time,
you are our defence and protection.

When your people were oppressed, down trodden, defeated,
your justice prevailed.
You sought us out in slavery,
You brought us out of exile,
You lowered the mountain,
raised the valley
and brought us home.

When your people turned to the gods of power and money,
ignorant of your Word
you were the dissenting voice.
You confront our faithlessness,
oppose the abuse of power,
and speak in the silence of the voiceless.

So now with the generations of people long gone,
but still present in the sacredness of memory;
with the martyrs and prophets of our day;
with all God's people in all the continents and throughout time
we sing:

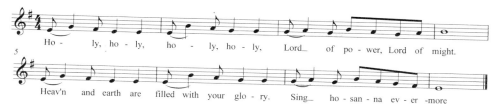

Holy, ho - ly, ho - ly, ho - ly, Lord of po - wer, Lord of might.

Heav'n and earth are filled with your glo - ry. Sing ho - san - na ev - er -more

(full music page 133)

**Holy, holy, holy, holy,
Lord of power, Lord of might.
Heaven and earth are filled with your glory.
Sing hosanna evermore.**

**Blest and holy, blest and holy,
He who comes from God on high.
Raise your voices, sing his glory,
Praise his name for evermore.**[3]

And now we acknowledge your coming,
through the creation of the world in the beauty of shape and the miracle of matter,
and to us in bread and wine.

through the mothers and fathers of faith in their story of exodus and exile,
and to us in bread and wine.

through the defiant prophets, proclaiming a path,
free from corruption and injustice,
and to us in bread and wine.

through John the Baptist announcing your coming,
through Mary who accepted your invitation in her womb,
remaining faithful to the cross and to the tomb,
and to us in bread and wine.

You came to them and you come to us,
making these gifts holy
and transforming them,
to be the body and blood of Jesus Christ,
Who on the night of his arrest,
betrayal and torture,
took bread,
blessed it,
broke it,
gave it to his disciples saying:

---

3   The "Israeli" Mass

"Take, eat, this is my body,
which is given for you.
Do this in remembrance of me."

In the same way also
He took the cup,
after supper, saying:
"This is my blood of the New Covenant
poured out for many, for the forgiveness of sins.
As often as you drink it,
do it in remembrance of me."

As often as you eat this bread and drink the cup,
you proclaim the Lord's death, until He comes.

We proclaim the mystery of faith:
Christ has died!
Christ is risen!
Christ will come again!

So in memory of all that Christ has done for us,
we bring our thanks to God.

May we be united
as your people,
in this place,
in this hour,
and with all people
in all places
and every hour.

May we live your sacrifice,
and share your death.

We stand in your presence,
free and forgiven,
alive and strong.

We remember all who have died in faith, especially those close to us;
they are alive in your love.

We remember all in need;
they are closest to your heart.

We pray for all who receive this sacrament;
that we may be strengthened and renewed.

We pray united with God and all creation,
empowered by the Holy Spirit,
liberated through the love of Jesus our friend and brother,
who has opened the kingdom for all to enter;
through whom,
with whom,
in whom,
in the unity of the Holy Spirit,
all glory and honour are yours,
almighty God,
now and forever.
AMEN!

The Lord's Prayer

The peace of the Lord be always with you.
And also with you!

(the peace is shared)

We break this bread so that we may share it.
In this broken body, we are one, each with the other.

Lamb of God, you take away the sin, the sin of all the world:
give us mercy, give us mercy, give us mercy Lamb of God.

(full music page 133)

Lamb of God, you take away the sin,
the sin of all the world:
give us mercy, give us mercy,
give us mercy, Lamb of God.

Lamb of God, you take away the sin,
the sin of all the world,
give us mercy, give us mercy,
give us mercy, Lamb of God.

Lamb of God, you take away the sin,
the sin of all the world:
grant us peace, Lord, grant us peace, Lord,
grant us peace, Lamb of God.[4]

4   The "Israeli" Mass

Holy things for holy people.
Only God is holy!

Distribution

God, you have come to us:
Lord Jesus, come.

God, the time is near:
Lord Jesus, come.

God, your people long for justice:
Lord Jesus, come.

God, we await your birth:
Lord Jesus, come.
AMEN!
HALLELUJAH!
AMEN!

Christmas

take, bless, break, give

Lighting the Christmas Candle

Once we walked in darkness.
Now we see a glorious light.

Once we lived in the shadow of death
Now the dawn has risen.

A large white candle is lit[5]
The Light of Christ
Thanks be to God!

Gloria, Gloria in excelsis Deo!
Gloria, Gloria, Alleluia, Alleluia![6]

Jesus Christ,
born this day,
come among us,
fill the heavens and the earth
with the songs of angels
and the prayers of the simple.
Enter this moment and this place with love,
so that we might know you here
in our weakness, vulnerability and joy,
and sense in the fragility of your birth
the future hope of humankind.
We pray in the name of the Babe of Bethlehem
loved of old, and worshipped today.
Amen

---

5 If the white candle is the centre of an advent wreath, the other four candles should be
   lit before the service starts.
6 Taizé

Christmas Eucharistic Prayer

These are our gifts of bread and wine.
We bring them to God.

We come ready to receive the God, who came at Christmas.
We come, with open hearts and longing souls.

Blessed be God!
Blessed be God forever!

The Lord be with you!
And also with you!

Lift up your hearts!
We lift them to the Lord!

Let us give thanks!
It is right to give God thanks and praise!

We praise you,
Powerful Creator of the universe.
**In the beginning
you were the Word,
which commanded life into being.**

We adore you
our God who kept the promise
made to our ancestors in faith –
a promise to redeem the earth
and set its people free.
**In the fullness of time,
You came to us in Jesus,
a baby, born of God's desire
to lift up the broken hearted.**

We worship You
with the simplicity of a shepherd's conviction
with the wise of ancient days,
who knelt before You and paid you homage.
**Come, Lord Jesus, come!
be born again in our hearts
and restore our broken spirits.**
In the company of generations of people,
present in the sacredness of memory,

with the martyrs and prophets of our day;
with all of God's people
in all the continents and throughout history,
with angels and archangels and all the company of heaven,
we sing:

(full music page 135)

Holy, holy, holy.
My heart, my heart adores You.
My heart is glad to say the words:
"You are holy, Lord."[7]

Blessed is the One who comes in the name of the Lord.
Hosanna in the highest.

→O God
We give thanks for your coming:
in the creation of the world,
the beauty of shape and the miracle of matter,
[and to us in bread and wine:]

to Mary and Joseph,
human parents at the heart of a universal story,
[and to us in bread and wine:]

to shepherds asleep on a hillside,
disturbed by the celebration of the cosmos at the rebirth of creation,
[and to us in bread and wine:]

through the wisdom of the East,
kneeling at the door of the stable,
gold, frankincense and myrrh in hand,
[and to us in bread and wine.]

You came to them and you come to us,   f. your sake.
transforming (these gifts) all things → 26
to be for us the body and blood of Jesus Christ,
Who on the night of his arrest,

---

7   Santo - Argentina

betrayal and torture
took bread,
blessed it,
broke it,
gave it to his disciples saying:
"Take, eat, this is my body,
which is given for you.
Do this in remembrance of me."

In the same way also
He took the cup,
after supper, saying:
"This is my blood of the New Covenant
poured out for many, for the forgiveness of sins.
As often as you drink it,
do it in remembrance of me."

As often as you eat this bread and drink the cup,
you proclaim the Lord's death, until he comes.

We proclaim the mystery of faith:
Christ has died!
Christ is risen!
Christ will come again!

So in memory of all that Christ has done for us,
through our faith day-by-day,
we bring our thanks to God.

May we be united
as your people,
in this place,
in this hour,
and with all people
in all places
and in every hour.

May we live your sacrifice,
and share your death.

We stand in your presence,
free and forgiven,
alive and strong.

We remember all who have died in faith, especially those close to us;
they are alive in your love.

We remember all in need;
they are closest to your heart.

We pray for all who receive this sacrament;
that we may be strengthened and renewed.

We pray united with God and all creation,
empowered by the Holy Spirit,
liberated through the love of Jesus our friend and brother,
who has opened the kingdom for all to enter;
through whom,
with whom,
in whom,
in the unity of the Holy Spirit,
all glory and honour are yours,
almighty God,
now and forever.
AMEN!

The Lord's Prayer

The peace of the Lord be always with you.
And also with you!

(We share the peace)

We break this bread
In sharing it, we are one, each with the other.

You are the Lamb of God,
who takes away the sin of the world.
Have mercy on us.

You are the Lamb of God
who takes away the sin of the world.
Have mercy on us

You are the Lamb of God
who takes away the sin of the world.
Give us peace.

Holy things for holy people.
Only God is holy.

Distribution

 From the company of each other
and our fellowship with all of God's People,
we have received,
grace upon grace.

 From this cup of blessing,
we have received,
grace upon grace.

 From the heart of our God,
Creator of the Universe,
Source of life and love,
Hope of the lost and the lonely,
we have received,
grace upon grace.

Thank you God
Thank you God for everything.

AMEN!
HALLELUJAH!
AMEN!

Eucharist on the Magnificat

(Particularly suitable for feasts of Mary, and occasions when we pray for social justice)

We bring bread baked with flour and yeast,
fruit of creation and human effort,
food for the body,
life for humanity.
Blessed be God forever!

We bring wine fermented from grapes,
fruit of creation and human effort,
drink for the thirsty,
hope for humanity.
Blessed be God forever!

God fills the hungry with good things,
the rich are sent empty away.
Blessed be God forever!

Let our souls magnify the Lord!
Our spirits rejoice in God, our Saviour!

Lift up your hearts!
We lift them to God!

Let us give thanks to God!
It is right to give God thanks and praise!

We rejoice in God
for the promise made
to our ancestors and their descendants:
God's promise always to help us -
always to show mercy
**Great is God's love,
love without end.**

We rejoice in God
for Mary, our mother,
first disciple of our brother Jesus,
who denounced oppression
and announced the Good News
that God has put down the powerful from their thrones
and scattered the proud in the imagination of their hearts.
**Great is God's love,
love without end.**

We rejoice in God,
that the impoverished,
the abused,
the landless,
the humble and the meek
are lifted up.
Great is God's love,
love without end.

We rejoice in God,
for the favour granted to the voiceless,
by their courage, their suffering,
their endurance, their resistance,
they have been blessed
and through them
the radiance of the cross of Christ revealed
from generation to generation.
Great is God's love,
love without end.

We rejoice in God,
for our ancestors
and those yet to be born.

We sing with all God's people,
believing in the transformation of the earth,
through the holiness of the Mighty One who does great things,
and the freedom of all God's children:

Ho - ly, Ho - ly, Ho - ly,___ Lord, God of Hosts.

Heaven and earth are full of your glo - ry Ho - sa - na in the high - est.

(full music page 136)

Holy, Holy, Holy,
Lord God of hosts,
Heaven and earth are full of your glory,
Hosanna in the highest! [8]

So in the company of the great cloud of witnesses,
in loyal and faithful communion with each other,
our thanksgiving is expressed in our sacred memory,
as we recall the moment of our salvation.

8 Melody – South Africa

Come, Holy Spirit, breathe into this moment.

We come closer to our God,
through the grieving faithfulness of Mary,
and our memory of Jesus,
Who on the night of his arrest,
betrayal and torture
took bread,
blessed it,
broke it,
gave it to his disciples saying:
"Take, eat, this is my body,
which is given for you.
Do this in remembrance of me."

In the same way also
He took the cup,
after supper, saying:
"This is my blood of the New Covenant
poured out for many, for the forgiveness of sins.
As often as you drink it,
do it in remembrance of me."

As often as you eat this bread and drink the cup,
you proclaim the Lord's death, until he comes.

So remembering your sacrifice,
made, once for all, upon the cross,
we offer our sacrifice to you.
Let it be with us, Lord,
according to your Word.

Overshadow us with your Spirit from on high.
Pour out your mighty and life-giving Spirit,
upon this bread and wine
and upon your people gathered here,
that they and we may be transformed
to be the Body and Blood of Christ,
here in the Assembly of Believers
and in the world.
Look, with favour upon your servants in our lowliness,
and bless the generations yet to be born.

We pray for the wretched of this earth:
for the downtrodden and neglected;
for those who defend human rights;
for those who protect the integrity and wholeness of creation;
for those imprisoned for truth;
for those who hunger and thirst for justice.

We offer this prayer of thanksgiving and sacrifice
in the name of Jesus,
through whom,
with whom,
in whom
in the unity of the Holy Spirit,
all glory and honour are yours,
almighty God,
now and forever.

A - men si - ya - ku - du - mis sa.   A - men si - ya - ku - du - mi - sa.

A - men ba - wo.   A - men ba wo.   a - men si - ya - ku - du - mis - sa.

(full music page 136)

Amen siakudumisa!
Amen siakudumisa!
Amen bawo. Amen bawo.
Amen siakudumisa![9]
Amen. Praise the name of the Lord.

The Lord's Prayer

The Peace of the Lord be always with you.
And also with you!

(The peace is shared)

We break this bread
In sharing it, we are one, each with the other.

9   South Africa - traditional

Be - hold the Lamb of God, be - hold the La - mb of God. Who takes a - way the sin, the - sin - of - the world.

(full music page 137)

Behold the Lamb of God,
Behold the Lamb of God,
Who takes away the sin,
The sin of the world.[10]

Holy things for holy people.
Only God is holy.

Distribution

As we leave this service of thanksgiving,
we return to the service of the Lord in the world.
Renewed by the story of your liberation,
strengthened by your promise,
empowered by the coming of your Spirit,
enriched by the communion of your church,
we offer thanks for all your grace has given,
so we may go out with joy,
to love and serve the Lord.

Go in peace.
May the God of peace go with you.

10 Iona

take, bless, break, give

Epiphany

take, bless, break, give

Epiphany

Collect

Jesus, nestling in a manger,
respected in reverence
by travellers, searching for truth,
reading the night sky, navigated by desire,
searching within and searching without,
following an Asian star,
coming to you,
carrying in their hands,
the fruits of eastern wisdom,
recognising the one unrecognised
by those he came to save,
and feared by rulers
whose tyranny is subverted by tenderness.

May we encounter You, our God,
in humility.
May we be transformed,
to wander home another Way,
open to new Truth
willing to receive your new Life.

Our prayer is offered in the name
of the Child of Bethlehem,
a refugee in Egypt.
Amen

Epiphany Eucharistic Prayer

These are our gifts of bread and wine.
We bring them to God.

These are our gifts of adoration and wonder.
We offer them to God.

These are our gifts of sacrifice and love.
We worship you, Christ the Lord.

The Lord be with you!
And also with you!

Lift up your hearts!
We lift them to the Lord!

Let us give thanks!
It is right to give God thanks and praise!

We praise you Creator of the heavens and the earth,
Light of the Cosmos,
Origin of all that is and all that will be.
From the beginning of time,
You have looked at your Creation
and known it to be good.

In the fullness of time, your Word was made flesh
and lived among us,
revealing in human shape
the formless God beyond and within all time and space.
We have seen your glory, full of grace and truth.

The light of your star was seen throughout the earth,
understood by the wise and the simple,
proclaiming the unity of all people in the power of God's spirit.
We have seen it too, and have to come to worship.

In your presence
and in the company of generations of people long gone, but present
in the sacredness of memory;
with the peoples of the Americas, of the Caribbean, of Asia and the
Pacific, of Africa and of Europe,
with our sisters and brothers of faith, searching for your light;
with all of God's people throughout time and space, we adore you,
we worship you and we sing:

(full music page 135)

**Holy, Holy, Holy,
my heart, my heart adores you,
my heart is glad to say the words:
"You are holy, Lord."**[11]

We know you to be the Creator of the world,
shaping life and giving form to the earth.

We thank you through our gifts, our talents, our commitment.

We know you to be the liberator of the world,
leading your children from slavery into freedom.

**We thank you through our gifts, our talents, our commitment,
our hunger for justice.**

We know you to be the sustenance of life, nurturing your children
with faith and hope.

**We thank you through our gifts, our talents, our commitment,
our hunger for justice, our desire for love.**

Through the wisdom of Asia, your infant Son was revealed to the
People of God;
through Joseph, your Child was saved from disappearance and
massacre;
through Mary, your Son was named as Saviour and held tight in
her arms, on the journey into African exile.

**We thank you through our gifts, our talents, our commitment,
our longing for freedom, our hunger for justice, our hope for
the world.**

---

11 Santo Argentina

Pour down your Spirit on these gifts and make them for us the body
and blood of Jesus Christ,
Who on the night of his arrest,
betrayal and torture
took bread,
blessed it,
broke it,
gave it to his disciples saying:
"Take, eat, this is my body,
which is given for you.
Do this in remembrance of me."

In the same way also
He took the cup,
after supper, saying:
"This is my blood of the New Covenant
poured out for many, for the forgiveness of sins.
As often as you drink it,
do it in remembrance of me."

As often as you eat this bread and drink the cup,
you proclaim the Lord's death, until he comes.

So we proclaim the mystery of faith:

Christ has died!
Christ is risen!
Christ will come again!

In memory of all that Christ has done for us,
we eat this bread and drink this wine,
meeting together as community, in communion with you.

You have set us free.
You are ours.
We are yours.

We pray for all in need,
the poor,
the hungry,
the mourning,
the persecuted.

We remember all who have died in faith, especially those close to us;
We pray that, through this sacrament, we may be strengthened
and renewed.

Our prayers unite us with those of former days
and those yet to be born,
with all creation and with God,
whose Kingdom is open for all to enter,
through Christ Jesus our Lord,
through whom,
with whom,
in whom
in the unity of the Holy Spirit,
all glory and honour are yours,
almighty God
now and forever.
AMEN!

The Lord's Prayer

The peace of the Lord be always with you.
And also with you!

(The peace is shared)

We break this bread so that we may share it.
In this broken body, we are one, each with the other.

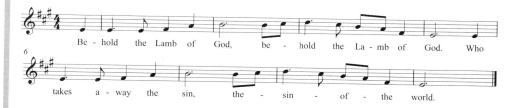

(full music page 137)

Behold the Lamb of God,
Behold the Lamb of God,
Who takes away the sin,
The sin of the world.

Holy things for holy people.
Only God is holy.

Distribution

Thank you for this hour,
Thank you for this feast,
Thank you for your presence
Thank you for the precious gift of Jesus Christ.
Help us to follow Him,
Help us to serve Him,
Help us to love Him,
as He loves us.

Go into the world, to love and to serve!
In the name of Christ, we go,
Amen!

Ordinary Time

take, bless, break, give

Ordinary Time

Prayers of healing

Declare your truth, Holy Spirit
to our troubled souls.
Look into our pain.
Gaze into our innermost being.
Let your wisdom penetrate our distress.

We name our failure to honour
the generations which lived before us
and to carry forward the visions of our ancestors.

We name our distress,
visited on us by those who wish us harm,
resentful and bitter enemies,
jealous and faithless friends.

We name our oppressors,
those who feel themselves superior,
the systems of gain and loss,
which impoverish and control,
discrimination, exploitation, racism.

Send down your Spirit upon us
make us courageous and strong,
refreshed and healed.
Through your power
save the world from darkness
from oppression, hatred and violence.

Liberating Spirit,
You can cleanse.
You can set us free.

Powerful Spirit:
claim your own,
come with healing,
come with love.

Pour down your judgement
on the powers and rulers of this earth.
Castigate the evildoers
and lift up the children of freedom,

Rest quietly,
unhappy spirits of our ancestors.
Accept forgiveness,
hurt spirits of our enemies.

Feel God's healing,
pained spirits of our sickness.

Go forever from this earth,
oppressive spirits of dominating powers.

God deliver us from evil.
God deliver us from evil.

Eucharistic Prayer

These are our gifts of bread and wine.
We bring them to God.

Here are our lives in need of healing.
We offer them to God.

Here are our hopes and dreams.
We seek fulfilment in Christ.

The Lord be with you!
And also with you!

Lift up your hearts!
We lift them to God!

It is just to give God thanks and praise!
It is just and right to do so!

It is with real joy
that we give You thanks.
You are the joy within us.

It is with real hope
that we give You thanks.
You are the hope before us.

It is with real peace
that we give You thanks.
Your peace surrounds us.

We praise you because
You lived your life with us.
You taught, healed, befriended
our broken humanity.
You placed yourself with the poor, the hungry,
the mourning and the persecuted.

Sit with us here
so we may learn from You
and be healed by You.

Unite us now with
the repentant,
the forgiving,
the loving,
of every generation
with the martyrs of every continent,
with our ancestors in faith
and with the choirs of heaven
with whom we join in an unending song of celebration:

(full music page 135)

Holy, holy, holy.
My heart, my heart adores You.
My heart is glad to say the words:
"You are holy, Lord."[12]

As your praise echoes
throughout the centuries,
we bring our thanks,
for Jesus, your Son,
praying His blessing on your Church, gathered here,
in love for each other and for You.

We give thanks for all who lived your Gospel story;
for Mary your mother,
your weak and brash disciples,
the crowds of the needy and the curious,
who heard your message
and believed,
who felt your touch
and were healed.

Bless this communion, which unites us with them.

---

12 Santo - Argentina

Bless this bread and wine,
that it become the body and blood of Jesus,
Who on the night of his arrest,
betrayal and torture
took bread,
blessed it,
broke it,
gave it to his disciples saying:
"Take, eat, this is my body,
which is given for you.
Do this in remembrance of me."

In the same way also
He took the cup,
after supper, saying:
"This is my blood of the New Covenant
poured out for many, for the forgiveness of sins.
As often as you drink it,
do it in remembrance of me."

As often as you eat this bread and drink the cup,
you proclaim the Lord's death, until he comes.

In your presence, we proclaim our faith in you:

Christ has died!
Christ is risen!
Christ will come again!

Accept our faith,
accept our love,
accept our very being.
You have given us all we have.
It is to you that we now return
with total commitment.

Remember all in need, all treated unjustly, all who are sick and
longing for peace.
Embrace them with compassion;
stretch out your healing hand.

We pray for ourselves as we minister to each other and to the world.
Have mercy on us.
Forgive us our wrong.

Remember all our families and friends
in so many parts of the world,
from whom we are separated.
**Enfold us in your love,
with those who have died
and remain precious in our memory.**

Together then we adore Christ Jesus,
visible image of the invisible God,
**through whom,
with whom,
in whom,
in the unity of the Holy Spirit,
all glory and honour are yours,
almighty God,
now and forever.
AMEN!**

The Lord's Prayer

Peace is the gift of God.
Peace is here for us to share.

The Peace of God be always with you
And also with you!

(we share the peace)

We break this bread so that we may share it.
In this broken body, we are one, each with the other.

Be - hold the Lamb of God, be - hold the La mb of God. Who

takes a - way the sin, the - sin - of - the world.

(full music page 137)

**Behold the Lamb of God,
Behold the Lamb of God,
Who takes away the sin,
The sin of the world.**[13]

---

13 Iona

Holy things for holy people.
Only God is holy.

Distribution

We came in fear.
We received your love.

We came in despair.
We received your joy.

We came in weakness.
We received your power.

We came laid low.
You lifted us up.

Go in the power of God.

God bless you.
And God bless you.

Celtic Eucharist[14]

In name of God,
In name of Son,
In name of Spirit,
Amen.

Perfect power,
Perfect love,
Perfect Three,
Amen.

Blessed aid,
Blessed guide,
Blessed Trinity,
Amen.

The blessing of God;
God of life and of the morning.
The peace of God;
God of life and of the noontide.
The shield of God;
God of life and of the evening.
The power of the Three;
God of life and of the night-time.

Face of God in the rising sun;
Eye of God in drops of water on an infant's brow;
Feet of God on the rough pathway of a pilgrim's journey.

Face of Christ in the full new moon;
Eye of Christ in the midnight of the tired, stumbling soul;
Hand of Christ in the drops of blood on the soil of freedom.

Glory, to the God of Life.

---

14 Based on traditional Celtic prayers – suitable for ordinary time and Trinity Sunday

You are holy, you are whole.
You are always ever more
than we ever understand.
You are always at hand.
Blessed are you coming near.
Blessed are you coming here
to your church in wine and bread,
raised from soil, raised from dead.
You are holy.
You are wholeness.
You are present.
Let the cosmos praise you Lord!
Hallelujah, Hallelujah, Hallelujah,
Hallelujah, our Lord[15]

Father, make us holy,
Saviour, shield us from sin,
Spirit, free us from guilt
gently and generously.

Grace our life with milk-honey yield.
Give us bread, yeast-fermenting life.
Grace our table with cream from the field.
Give us wine, fruit-fermenting love.

15 Per Harling - Sweden

Christ of ancient days,
Christ of newborn days,
Christ of the Upper room,
Bless our days with Christ protecting succour.

Christ cherish us
as you cherished your disciples
in the upper room.
On the night of your arrest,
betrayal and torture.
You took bread,
blessed it,
broke it,
gave it to his disciples saying:
"Take, eat, this is my body,
which is given for you.
Do this in remembrance of me."

Bread-taking night,
Blessing, taking and sharing with friends.

In the same way also,
You took the cup,
after supper, saying:
"This is my blood of the New Covenant
poured out for many, for the forgiveness of sins.
As often as you drink it,
do it in remembrance of me."

Wine-taking night,
blessing and giving for all the world.

As often as you eat this bread and drink the cup,
you proclaim the Lord's death, until he comes.

Eat and drink with friends in the Body of Christ.
With those lost to us.
With Saints of ancient days,
With the journeying, wilderness-surviving, promised land-arriving,
Pilgrim People of God.

Encircle your people with warmth of the hearth.
Encircle your people with love of the heart.
Encircle your people, with dreams of food for all.
Encircle your people with a voice and a call.
Christ, our en-circler.

Peace of God between friend and lover.
Peace of God between parent and child.
Peace of God between sisters and brothers.
Peace of God in strife torn neighbours.
Peace of God in battle scarred lands.

Peace of God in hungry and lonely.
Peace of God in mind-created prisons.
Peace of God in human-injustice, human-cruelty, human-stumbling,
human-weariness.
Christ, our peace.

Peace be to you my neighbour.
Peace be to you my friend.

Pain of Christ within our caring
Pain of Christ within our daring
Pain of Christ within our hoping
Christ, sacrifice, lost that all be found.
Christ, our Passover.

Christ of the poor within our sharing.
Christ of the poor within our feasting.
Christ of the poor within our loving.
Christ of the poor, heart of our God.

Chief of the Heavens.
Glorious Trinity
Strength of our Purpose.
Amen

The Lord's Prayer

Be - hold the Lamb of God, be - hold the La - mb of God. Who takes a - way the sin, the - sin - of - the world.

Behold the Lamb of God,
Behold the Lamb of God,
Who takes away the sin,
The sin of the world.[16]

(full music page 137)

---

16 Iona

Holy things for holy people.
Only God is holy

Distribution

With us here in breaking of bread.
With us here now we have fed.
Protect our body from fear and pain.
May we go on, in Christ to gain.

Christ be with us, Christ with-in us, Christ be-hind us, Christ be-fore us, Christ be-side us, Christ to win us, Christ to com-fort and re-store us, Christ be-neath us, Christ a-bove us, Christ in qui-et, Christ in dan-ger, Christ in hearts of all that love us, Christ in mouth of friend and stran-ger.

(full music page 138)

Christ be with us, Christ within us,
Christ behind us, Christ before us,
Christ beside us, Christ to win us,
Christ to comfort and restore us.
Christ beneath us, Christ above us,
Christ in quiet, Christ in danger,
Christ in hearts of all that love us,
Christ in mouth of friend and stranger.[17]

Bind to yourself, Trinity's name.
Go in peace, in the love of Jesus, Mary's Son.

Trinity's name, our protector:
Amen, Amen, Amen.

---

17 Attributed to St Patrick

Lent
Lent
Lent

take, bless, break, give

Kyrie

When we are hiding:
Lord have mercy.

When we are denying:
Christ have mercy.

When we are betraying:
Lord have mercy.

Ash Wednesday – imposition of ashes

Have mercy on us O God.

**Have mercy on us, O God,
according to your steadfast love;**

Life is sorrow,
Life is pain,
Life is confronted by death.

**According to your abundant mercy,
blot out my transgressions.**

World is sorrow,
World is pain,
World is confronted by death.

**Wash me thoroughly from my iniquity,
and cleanse me from my sin.**[18]

Life is defeated,
Life is polluted,
Life is crushed,
Life is confronted by death.

**For we know our transgressions,
and our sin is ever before us.**[19]

Corruption is before us,
Pain is before us,
Sickness is before us,
Sorrow is before us,
Death is before us.

**The sacrifice acceptable to God is a broken spirit.
A broken and contrite heart, O God, You will not despise.**[20]

Break us,
for love of your world.
Renew us,
for love of your people.
Confront us,
and make our sacrifice complete.

---

18 Psalm 51 v 1f (NRSV)
19 Psalm 51 v 15 (NRSV)
20 Psalm 51 v 17 (NRSV)

A cross of ashes is marked on the forehead of each person with the words
> **Remember you are dust,**
> **And it is to dust that you shall return.**

Help us, O God,
to live our lives, in remembrance of your death.
Help us, O God,
to die our death with your love in our hearts
and your name on our lips.
Help us, O God,
to honour your sacrifice,
through our openness
to healing in the time of our brokenness
and may our lives be constantly devoted to your service.

Create in us a clean heart, O God,
and put a new and right spirit within us.
Do not cast us away from your presence,
and do not take your Holy Spirit from us.
Restore to us the joy of your salvation
and sustain in us a willing spirit.[21]

---

21 Psalm 51 10-12 (NRSV)

Prayer

When we sink into the water,
hold us firm.
When we rise to new life,
set us free.

When we face the cross,
heal our sorrow.
When we walk to the tomb,
open our joy.

When the moon gives only darkness,
may we abandon our fear.
When the sun rises in the east,
may we share the broken bread
with all humanity.

Lenten Eucharistic Prayer

Bread and wine are our offering.
Bread and wine are our love.

Bread and wine are our sorrow.
**Bread and wine are our sharing of God
and with each other.**

The Lord be with you!
And also with you!

May Jesus our brother accompany us on our journey.
and strengthen us in love.

Lift up your hearts!
We lift them to God!

Let us give thanks to God!
It is right to give God thanks and praise!

We give thanks to God,
who created us,
who saved us from the flood,
who delivered the people from slavery and led them to freedom.
We boldly approach the holy God.

We give thanks to God for Jesus,
who lived our life with us,
our great High Priest, who passed through the heavens,
tempted in all things as are we,
able to sympathise with our weakness,
tried and tested but remaining without sin.
We ask for mercy and grace in our time of need.

We give thanks for the mercy shown
to God's people , through the ever-present Spirit of God:
lifting us up when we are low,
carrying our burden when we are crushed,
wakening dreams of home in exile,
transforming weapons of war into instruments of peace.
Holy God, have mercy on us.

Holy God – be with us now.

(full music page 133)

Holy, holy, holy, holy,
Lord of power, Lord of might.
Heaven and earth are filled with your glory.
Sing hosanna evermore.

Blest and holy, blest and holy.
He who comes from God on high.
Raise your voices, sing his glory,
Praise his name for evermore.[22]

God is holy indeed.
Truly holy.

Truly holy,
And truly present in this moment.

Your name is holy,
from the rising of the sun to its setting.

In every corner of the earth,
God's name is praised.

In every corner of the earth,
God's people struggle for justice.

In every corner of the earth,
God's people seek a true and lasting peace.

In this corner of the earth,
we name you as our Saviour.
offering you our imperfect lives,
that they may be perfected
through your love.

22 The "Israeli" Mass

And now Father God,
we ask you to send your Spirit upon this bread and wine,
our offering of love and freedom.
Make them for us the body and blood of Jesus, our brother,
Who on the night of his arrest,
betrayal and torture
took bread,
blessed it,
broke it,
gave it to his disciples saying:
"Take, eat, this is my body,
which is given for you.
Do this in remembrance of me."

In the same way also
He took the cup,
after supper, saying:
"This is my blood of the New Covenant
poured out for many, for the forgiveness of sins.
As often as you drink it,
do it in remembrance of me."

As often as you eat this bread and drink the cup,
you proclaim the Lord's death, until he comes.

Now we taste your freedom,
even in the midst of suffering and oppression.
**We stand at the foot of your cross,
your disciples forever.**

As we remember your suffering on the cross,
we pray for:
the disappeared,
the tortured,
the betrayed,
the broken,
the grieving.

We witness the brutality of sin
and the power of love to overcome it.
Grieving for our world,
we come together in communion with all the people of God
and in celebration of God's love among us.

So may we who receive this bread and wine,
through your Spirit,
live forever in communion with the Saviour,
through his reconciling blood,
sharing his passion for human peace and justice.

In God's love, we pray:
for peace between your people.
Lord, have mercy.

For reconciliation of conflict
and peace in the world.
Christ, have mercy.

For strength and wisdom
in those who are restless for your Kingdom,
Lord, have mercy.

We pray for all who have died:
for our ancestors in faith;
saints and martyrs of every
generation and continent.
We pray for those who we have loved,
from whom we are separated by the great divides of sea and death,
and pray to be united with them,
in this Holy Communion,
in which, through your grace,
we now share.

These prayers we offer in the name of Jesus,
through whom,
with whom,
in whom,
in the unity of the Holy Spirit,
all glory and honour are yours,
almighty God,
now and forever.
AMEN!

The Lord's Prayer

Peace, Peace be with you.
And also with you!

(We share the peace)

We are many,
and yet we all share in the one bread.

Lamb of God, you take a - way the sin, the sin of all the world:
give us mer - cy, give us mer - cy, give us mer - cy Lamb of God.

(full music page 133)

**Lamb of God, you take away the sin,
the sin of all the world:
give us mercy, give us mercy:
give us mercy, Lamb of God.**

**Lamb of God, you take away the sin,
the sin of all the world:
give us mercy, give us mercy,
give us mercy, Lamb of God.**

**Lamb of God, you take away the sin,
the sin of all the world:
grant us peace, Lord; grant us peace, Lord;
grant us peace, Lamb of God.**[23]

Holy things for holy people.
Only God is holy.

23 The "Israeli" Mass

Distribution

We have been fed with the body and blood of Jesus.
We will walk with him to Calvary.

We have grown closer to each other.
We will carry each other's burden.

We have witnessed the coming Kingdom.
We will walk in the light of God.

The new dawn is coming.
We believe it to be true.

Maundy Thursday

take, bless, break, give

Maundy Thursday

Lighting of the Festival Candles

This series of prayers introduces the Easter Liturgy. The service should begin at sunset. It begins as a Festival Service but is interrupted in order that the story of the Last Supper, arrest, trial and crucifixion can be told before resuming the Gloria on Easter Sunday morning.

A seven-branched candlestick is on the central table. A mother of the congregation lights the candles.

She prays:

> Blessed are you, O Lord, our God,
> King of the universe,
> Who has sanctified us by the commandments
> And has commanded us to kindle the festival lights.[24]

We sing:

When Israel was in Egypt's land – Rejoice and Sing 643

In this festival we commemorate the deliverance of God's people from evil. The angel of death passed over them. They were led by God's hand to freedom.

God holds our hands and leads us through death to life.

Gloria, gloria in excelsis deo,
Gloria, gloria, alleluia, alleluia.

---

24 From the Jewish Passover ceremony

The church bell or a temple gong sounding the angelus interrupts the singing of the Gloria, beginning *ff* but reducing in volume and intensity.

Silence

Far be it for me to glory except in the cross of our Lord Jesus Christ, by which the world has been crucified to me, and I to the world.[25]

God of the Passover,
you led us from slavery,
through the wilderness
and into the Promised Land.
Be with us at the beginning of our festival time,
as we face the wilderness of our world.
Keep before us:
the promise of your freedom,
the dream of your resurrection,
the anguish of your people.

A young child asks the question – the congregation respond.

Why is this night different from all other nights?
On this night there is no yeast in the bread we share.

Why is this night different from all other nights?
On this night, we eat bitter herbs.

Why is this night different from all other nights?[26]
On this night, we pray in the darkness as Jesus prayed.

(It is possible for each member of the congregation to take two small pieces of matzah and dip it in horseradish to eat as a sandwich, or dip a piece of fresh parsley in salt water and eat. The horseradish and matzah remind us that we eat unleavened bread and bitter herbs at the Passover (Numbers 9:11). The parsley represents the hyssop used to daub blood on the door posts (Exodus 12:22). Salt water represents the tears of suffering in slavery.)

---

25 Galatians 6: 14 (RSV)
26 Adapted from the Jewish Passover ceremony

Maundy Thursday
Maundy Thursday

Maundy Thursday Eucharistic Prayer and Tenebrae

Unleavened bread (Matzah or wafers) should be used.

This is the bread of affliction, which our forebears ate in the land of Egypt.
Come all who know hunger, come and eat.
All who are needy, come and share in the Passover,
this year here, next year in Jerusalem,
this year enslaved, next year as children of the free.[27]
Blessed be God forever!

The Lord be with you!
And also with you!

Lift up your hearts!
We lift them to God!

It is just to give God thanks and praise!
It is just and right to do so!

We give thanks to the living God,
Creator of the Universe,
who brought the world into being,
sun and star, moon and earth,
time, energy, form and matter,
sea, soil, wind and fire,
from the earliest of times
to the last moment of being.

We give thanks for our freedom in Christ.
We acknowledge liberation given to our forebears in slavery.
We give thanks for the homecomings of exiles
and the restoration of peace in war-torn lands.
We give thanks that your powerful arm held firm our ancestors
and continues to protect us today.
We give thanks that we can feel your hand upon our shoulders
making light our burden and lifting the weights from our backs.

We give thanks for our Saviour Jesus
Who on this sacred night
gave us this sacrament that in it
we might ever know the living God.
We thank you for the comfort it gives us,

---

27 Traditional Passover Prayer

the challenge it poses,
the vision it provokes,
the grace it imparts.

We thank you for the symbols of bread and wine
made with human hands and work,
baked and fermented with care.
Even though it is by human hate the bread is fractured,
and by human greed the blood is spilt,
we know through God's wounded hands,
our freedom will be won.

We give thanks
in deep communion
with all who struggle for your justice,
throughout the ages;
with the martyrs of our day;
the saints of ages past,
Mary our mother,
who for us accompanied the way of the cross,
and the messengers of God,
in every faith and place,
we join together to sing:

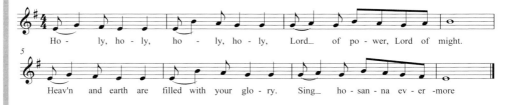

Ho - ly, ho - ly, ho - ly, ho - ly, Lord of po - wer, Lord of might.

Heav'n and earth are filled with your glo - ry. Sing ho - san - na ev - er -more

(full music page 133)

Holy, holy, holy, holy,
Lord of power, Lord of might.
Heaven and earth are filled with your glory.
Sing hosanna evermore.

Blest and holy, blest and holy,
He who comes from God on high.
Raise your voices, sing his glory,
Praise his name for evermore.[28]

---

28 The "Israeli" Mass

Blessed are you for on this night,
different from all other nights,
we remember your people,
wandering towards the promised land.
And on this night,
different from all other nights,
our Saviour Jesus,
stooped to wash the feet of his disciples,
endured betrayal,
arrest,
and torture,
took bread,
blessed it,
broke it,
gave it to his disciples saying:
"Take, eat, this is my body,
which is given for you.
Do this in remembrance of me."

In the same way also
He took the cup,
after supper, saying:
"This is my blood of the New Covenant
poured out for many, for the forgiveness of sins.
As often as you drink it,
do it in remembrance of me."

As often as you eat this bread and drink the cup,
you proclaim the Lord's death, until he comes.

**Lord we believe,
help our unbelief.**

We bring to mind Christ's suffering and death,
his prayerful agony in the garden.
With him we watch and pray for the Kingdom of God to come in our
lives and in our world, for the sake of the poor and the downtrodden.
As we participate in the memorial of Christ's sacrifice of himself for
the freedom of all,
We commit ourselves to the love of the earth,
and all its inhabitants,
praying that we might live together in the love of the crucified God
and accept the cost of discipleship.

Pour down your Spirit upon this bread and wine,
transform them to be for us the body and blood of our Saviour
Jesus Christ.
With your Spirit anoint your people gathered here
and all humankind
that Good News be preached to the poor,
release proclaimed to the captives,
recovery of sight to the blind,
and the transformation of humanity be complete.

Come, Lord Jesus, come.

We ask these prayers in the name of Christ Jesus,
through whom,
with whom,
in whom,
in the unity of the Holy Spirit,
all glory and honour are yours,
almighty God
now and forever.
AMEN!

As you prayed alone in the garden, so we pray for your kingdom
to come,
that your suffering will transform our bitter world
and your love conquer hatred and darkness.

The Lord's Prayer

We are many,
And yet we all share in the one bread.

Lamb_ of God, you take_ a - way the sin,__ the sin of all the world: give_ us mer - cy, give_ us mer - cy, give_ us mer - cy Lamb of God.

(full music page 133)

**Lamb of God, you take away the sin,
the sin of all the world:
give us mercy, give us mercy,
give us mercy, Lamb of God.**

**Lamb of God, you take away the sin,
the sin of all the world:
give us mercy, give us mercy,
give us mercy, Lamb of God.**

**Lamb of God, you take away the sin,
the sin of all the world:
grant us peace, Lord; grant us peace, Lord;
grant us peace, Lamb of God.**[29]

Holy things for holy people.
Only God is holy.

Distribution

The church is stripped of all ornaments.

The lights are lowered save for the seven candles.

When they had sung the hymn, they went out to the Mount of Olives.
Then Jesus said to them. "You will all become deserters because of
me this night; for it is written.
"I will strike the Shepherd,
and the sheep of the flock will be scattered."
But after I am raised up , I will go ahead of you to Galilee. Peter said
to him, "Though all become deserters because of you. I will never
desert you." Jesus said to him, "Truly I tell you, this very night,
before the cock crows, you will deny me three times." Peter said to
him, "Even though I must die with you, I will not deny you." And so
said all the disciples.[30]

---

29 The "Israeli" Mass
30 Matthew 26:30-35 NRSV

One candle is put out.

Lord, have mer - cy Lord,_ have mer - cy Lord,_ have mer - cy on us all.

Lord,_ have mer - cy Lord,_ have mer - cy Lord,_ have mer -cy -on us all.

(full music page 133)

Lord have mercy, Lord have mercy,
Lord have mercy on us all.
Lord have mercy, Lord have mercy,
Lord have mercy on us all.[31]

Out of the depths I cried to you O Lord;
Lord, hear my voice;
Let your ears consider well the voice of my supplication.

I wait for the Lord, my soul waits for him;
In his word there is hope.

My soul waits for the Lord, more than the night watch for the morning,
More than the night watch for the morning. [32]

A second candle is put out

Hear my voice, O God, in my complaint;
Preserve my life from fear of the enemy.

Hide me from the conspiracy of the wicked,
From the gathering of evildoers.

They sharpen their tongue like a sword,
And aim their bitter words like arrows.

They search out wickedness and lay a cunning trap,
For deep are the inward thoughts of the heart. [33]

A third candle is put out

---

31 Israeli Mass
32 Psalm 130 Common Worship
33 Psalm 64 Common Worship

Christ, have mer - cy, Christ, have mer - cy, Christ have mer - cy on us all.

Christ, have mer - cy, Christ have mer - cy, Christ, have mer - cy on us all.

Christ have mercy, Christ have mercy,
Christ have mercy on us all.
Christ have mercy, Christ have mercy,
Christ have mercy on us all.

(full music page 133)

Rescue me from my enemies, O my God;
Set me high above those that rise up against me.

Save me from the evildoers,
And from murderous foes deliver me.

For see how they lie in wait for my soul,
And the mighty stir up trouble against me.[34]

A fourth candle is put out

Have mercy on me, O God, for they trample over me;
All day long they assault and oppress me.

My adversaries trample over me all the day long;
Many are they that make proud war against me.

In the day of my fear I put my trust in you,
In God whose word I praise.

In God I trust, and will not fear
For what can flesh do to me?

A fifth candle is put out

I am alarmed at the voice of the enemy
And at the clamour of the wicked;

For they would bring evil upon me
And are set against me in fury.

My heart is disquieted within me,
And the terrors of death have fallen upon me.

---

34 Psalm 59 Common Worship

Fearfulness and dread are come upon me,
And a horrible dread has overwhelmed me.

And I said: "O that I had wings like a dove,
For then would I fly away and be at rest.

"Then would I flee far away
and make my lodging in the wilderness.

"I would make haste to escape
from the stormy wind and the tempest." 35

A sixth candle is put out.

Lord, have mer - cy Lord,_ have mer - cy Lord,_ have mer - cy on us all.

Lord,_ have mer - cy Lord,_ have mer - cy Lord,_ have mer -cy -on us all.

Lord have mercy, Lord have mercy
Lord have mercy on us all.
Lord have mercy, Lord have mercy
Lord have mercy on us all.36

(full music page 133)

O Lord, God of my salvation,
I have cried day and night before you.

Let my prayer come into your presence;
Incline your ear to my cry.

For my soul is full of troubles;
My life draws near to the land of death.

I am counted as one gone down to the Pit;
I am like one that has no strength,

Lost among the dead,
Like the slain who lie in the grave,

Whom you remember no more,
For they are cut off from your hand.

---

35 Psalm 55 Common Worship
36 Israeli Mass

I am so fast in prison that I cannot get free;
My eyes fail from all my trouble.

Lord, why have you rejected my soul?
Why have you hidden your face from me?

I have been wretched and at the point of death from my youth;
I suffer your terrors and am no more seen.

Your wrath sweeps over me;
Your horrors are come to destroy me;

All day long they come about me like water;
They close me in on every side.

Lover and friend have you put far from me
And my one companion is darkness.[37]

The remaining candle is extinguished and in darkness we sing;

(full music page 133)

**Lord have mercy, Lord have mercy,
Lord have mercy on us all.
Lord have mercy, Lord have mercy,
Lord have mercy on us all.**

**Christ have mercy, Lord have mercy,
Christ have mercy on us all.
Christ have mercy, Lord have mercy,
Christ have mercy on us all.**

**Lord have mercy, Lord have mercy,
Lord have mercy on us all.
Lord have mercy, Lord have mercy,
Lord have mercy on us all.**[38]

*The service concludes in darkness and silence – the congregation praying
and leaving when they are ready.*

---

37 Psalm 88 Common Worship (last line amended)
38 The "Israeli" Mass

take, bless, break, give

Maundy Thursday
Maundy Thursday
Maundy Thursday

Easter

take, bless, break, give

Easter

Lighting the Easter Candle

In the beginning, when God created the heavens and the earth, the earth was a formless void and darkness covered the face of the deep, while a wind from God swept over the face of the waters. And God said, "let there be light"; and there was light.[39]
Spirit of God, come, and re-create us.

Then the Lord said to Moses: "Why do you cry out to me? Tell the Israelites to go forward. But you lift up your staff, and stretch out your hand over the sea and divide it, that the Israelites may go into the sea on the dry land."[40]
Spirit of God, come, and set us free.

For a brief moment, I abandoned you, but with great compassion, I will gather you. In overflowing wrath, for a moment I hid my face from you, but with everlasting love I will have compassion on you, says the Lord, your Redeemer.
This is like the days of Noah to me. Just as I swore that the waters of Noah would never again go over the earth so I have sworn that I will not be angry with you and will not rebuke you.[41]
Spirit of God, come, and be our God.

O dry bones, hear the Word of the Lord. Thus says the Lord God to these bones: I will cause breath to enter you, and you shall live. I will lay sinews on you, and will cause flesh to come upon you and cover you with skin, and put breath in you, and you shall live, and you shall know that I am the Lord.[42]
Spirit of God, come, and give us life.

Christ, yesterday, today and tomorrow,
beginning and end,
Alpha and Omega,
all power is yours
time and eternity belong to you,
Great Ancestor of our Ancestors,
Age of all Ages,
for ever and for ever.
AMEN

---

39 Genesis 1 1-2 (NRSV)
40 Exodus 14 15-16 (NRSV)
41 Isaiah 54. 7-9 (NRSV)
42 Ezekiel 37.4b-6 (NRSV)

The Pascal Candle is lit

The light of Christ !
Thanks be to God!

The Lord is risen
(Shout)
HE IS RISEN INDEED!

Al - le - lu - jah, the Lord is ri sen. Al - le - lu - jah, He is ri - sen in deed.

(full music page 140)

Alleluia, the Lord is risen!
Alleluia, he is risen indeed![43]

Lift up your hearts!
We lift them to the Lord!

Rejoice, heavenly powers,
Rejoice, martyrs of the faith,
Rejoice, ancestors in glory
Rejoice, People of God.
Rejoice, for death is no more.
The Lord is risen!
HE IS RISEN INDEED!

Glo - ri - a, glo - ri - a, in ex - cel - sis Deo - o!

Glo - ri - a, glo - ri - a! Al - le - lu - ia! Al - le - lu - ia!

Gloria, Gloria, in excelsis Deo,
Gloria, Gloria. Alleluia, Alleluia!

---

43 Source unknown

Give thanks to the Lord, for he is good.
God's steadfast love, endures for ever.

Sing the songs of victory.
The right hand of God does valiantly.
The right hand of God is victorious.
The right hand of God does valiantly.

I shall not die, but I shall live
and tell the deeds of the Lord.
I thank you that you have answered me
and have become my salvation.

The stone that the builders rejected has become the cornerstone.

This is the Lord's song,
And it is marvellous in our eyes.

This is the day that the Lord has made;
Let us rejoice and be glad in it.[44]

---

44 Extracts from Psalm 118

Easter Eucharistic Prayer

(During an offertory hymn, gifts of money, Easter foods of eggs, milk and honey and Bread and Wine are brought forward)

God gave us food for the journey.
God gives food for our arriving.
God promised a Kingdom-feast,
God gives us milk and honey in the promised land,
and bread and wine
to recognise the risen Saviour.
Blessed be God for ever!

The Lord is here!
God's Spirit is with us!

Lift up your hearts!
We lift them to God!

Let us give thanks to God!
It is right to give God thanks and praise!

We give you thanks
that all things have been created,
through your renewing Spirit.

**Through your love
our Saviour was born.**

Through your compassion,
Christ lived among us,
the sick were healed,
and the dead brought to life.

**Through your grace,
He died our death.**

Through your justice,
he stood with the excluded,
and suffered with those who long for justice.

**Through your power,
He defeated death,**

Christ broke the chains of the oppressor,
lifts the hearts of his defeated disciples,
destroys the powers of hell.

**He opens the gate of His kingdom
for all people to enter.**

So with all who have lived in the faith of the crucified and risen Saviour,
all martyrs for the Kingdom,
all striving for God's justice and peace,
all who channel God's love and grace,
we join in their everlasting song:

(full music page 135)

**Holy, holy, holy.
My heart, my heart adores you.
My heart is glad to say the words:
"You are holy, Lord!"**[45]

You are holy,
and in your holiness,
we sense your Spirit.

Come in power
and make us your people.
Come, Spirit, come.

May these gifts of bread and wine be to us the body and blood of
Jesus Christ,
Who on the night of his arrest,
betrayal and torture
took bread,
blessed it,
broke it
gave it to his disciples saying:
"Take, eat, this is my body,
which is given for you.
Do this in remembrance of me."

---

45 Santo – Argentina

In the same way also
He took the cup,
after supper, saying:
"This is my blood of the New Covenant
poured out for many, for the forgiveness of sins.
As often as you drink it,
do it in remembrance of me."

As often as you eat this bread and drink the cup,
you proclaim the Lord's death, until he comes.

Our hearts burn within us.
We recognize you here, in the breaking of bread.

Now we see meaning in your death;
we look forward with joy to your final glory;
and we pray for your kingdom to come;

We give thanks that we can feast with you
and with all God's children in the banquet of life;
that we can share in the mystery of your being
through this resurrection meal.

Pour down your Spirit upon this Assembly of your people,
May we be gathered into your Kingdom,
and share this bread and this cup,
with the poor, the hungry, the mourning, the persecuted,
with all the saints, of every age and continent,
with those we have loved and who have died,
and now live in your eternal life.

We pray for the world at war,
Give us peace

We pray for the poor, downtrodden and abused.
Give them justice.

We pray for the bereaved and the dying.
Give them rest.

We pray for the people of God.
May the resurrection direct our lives:
forever praising you, from whom all good things come
and in whom we entrust our hope and invest our dreams.
This we ask in the name of Jesus, our Risen Lord,

**through whom,
with whom,
in whom
in the unity of the Holy Spirit,
all glory and honour are yours,
almighty God,
now and forever.
AMEN!**

The Lord's Prayer

The peace of the Lord be always with you.
And also with you!

(We share the peace)

We are many,
And yet we all share in the one bread.

Holy things for holy people.
Only God is holy.

Distribution

Al - le - lu - ia.   Al - le - lu - ia.   Al - le - lu - ia.   Al -

-lu - ia   Al - le - lu - ia. Al - le - lu - ia. El Sen - or re - us - ci - to

(full music page 139)

**Alleluia, Alleluia,
Alleluia, Alleluia,
Alleluia, Alleluia,
El Senor resucito.**[46]
(Alleluia, the Lord is risen)

---

46 Honduras arrangement John Bell

Risen Lord,
our liberator,
our companion,
our God,
we have been lifted up, we have been turned around.
You placed our feet on the solid ground.

We will go out into the world,
to live your praise in all we do.

Alleluia!
Alleluia!
Alleluia!
Praise God for our Risen Lord!
Praise God for resurrection in our lives!
Praise God for the victory belongs to the downtrodden!

The powers of this earth have been shaken from their thrones!
(Shout)
Alleluia!
Alleluia!
Alleluia!

Go in peace to love and serve the Lord!
In the name of Christ
AMEN!

Ascension

take, bless, break, give

Opening Prayer and Gloria

No longer visible, our love departs.
No longer shaped in human dress,
invisible and formless,
seated outside imagination,
above and beyond all time and space.
Give glory, give praise.

Glo - ri - a, glo - ri - a, in ex - cel - sis Deo - o!

Glo - ri - a, glo - ri - a! Al - le - lu - ia! Al - le - lu - ia!

Gloria, gloria, in excelsis deo.
Gloria, gloria, alleluia, alleluia.[47]

No longer alone, your disciples here.
Knowing You present, trusting your love,
invisible but real,
living in our hearts,
above and beyond all time and space.
Give glory, give praise.

We sing:

Gloria, gloria, in excelsis deo.
Gloria, gloria, alleluia, alleluia.

No longer grieving, we wait on you.
Knowing you will stay with us,
promised as a comforter,
promised in the breathing of the Spirit,
within and among all time and space.
Give glory, give praise.

---

47 Taizé

Gloria, gloria, in excelsis deo.
Gloria, gloria, alleluia, alleluia.

Alleluia!
Ascended Lord,
accept now our Gloria
and may it join with all
who sing your praise
above and beyond,
within and among all time and space.

We sing:

Gloria, gloria, in excelsis deo.
Gloria, gloria, alleluia, alleluia.

Ascension Eucharistic Prayer

The Lord is here!
God's Spirit is with us!

Lift up your hearts!
We lift them to God!

Let us give thanks to God!
It is right to give God thanks and praise!

We give thanks for our Saviour,
risen from the tomb,
who was revealed,
to his disciples
in a garden,
on a seashore,
on a dusty road,
in an upper room,
opening his hands
in blessing,
His wounds still fresh,
their wounds still to be healed.
Alleluia!
Risen Lord!

We give thanks for the believers
who with their risen friend,
on a hillside,
minds opened,
witnessing your leaving,
eyes gazing to heaven,
their sight clouding over,
visible image vanishing . . .
looking deep into their hearts,
and deeper into their souls,
waiting for the unseen Spirit,
in the depth, the very depth of their being
 - waiting
for the Spirit he promised to send.
Alleluia!
Ascended Lord!

We give thanks that we are here,
in your presence,
Ascended Lord of all glory.
For now you are seated in the heavens
beyond time,
beyond space,
beyond race,
creed,
class,
or tongue,
infinitely strong,
supremely wise.
Alleluia!
Jubilant Lord of Jubilee!

In trepidation,
worship,
wonder,
we come close to your throne
this touching stone
of grace,
compassion,
forgiveness,
love,
with all the tribes of humanity,
women, men,
young, old,
saints of ancient days,
the angels in the heavens,
orbiting planets and stars,
singing your eternal and unchanging praise:

Ho - ly, ho - ly ho - ly, my heart, my heart a - dores you! My heart is glad to say the - words you are ho - ly Lord.

(full music page 135)

Holy, holy, holy.
My heart, my heart adores you!
My heart is glad to say the words;
"You are holy, Lord!"[48]

48 Santo - Argentina

In their company,
we pray for your Spirit to descend,
coming from the clouds,
to which you have ascended,
coming to this bread
and this wine,
coming to your lonely and bewildered disciples
gathered here, today,
waiting here, today,
for your love to flow,
your grace to heal.

In our waiting,
we rest in Jesus, relying and trusting in the One,
Who on the night of his arrest,
betrayal and torture
took bread,
blessed it,
broke it,
gave it to his disciples saying:
"Take, eat, this is my body,
which is given for you.
Do this in remembrance of me."

In the same way also
He took the cup,
after supper, saying:
"This is my blood of the New Covenant
poured out for many, for the forgiveness of sins.
As often as you drink it,
do it in remembrance of me."

As often as you eat this bread and drink the cup,
you proclaim the Lord's death, until he comes.

**Your love has been poured out for us
and we believe.
No longer looking to the clouds,
but knowing you here.**

We pray:
for all who need your Spirit,
for all who need your healing,
for all who need your strength,
for all who have passed through life to death and now rest in
  your love.
Accept our offering, which we make in memory of you,
refresh our lives through the sharing of this sacrament,
unite us with your broken body,
that our pride might be broken too
and we know your risen power.

We ask this prayer
in the name of Jesus,
crucified,
risen,
ascended,
through whom,
with whom,
in whom,
in the unity of the Holy Spirit,
all glory and honour are yours,
almighty God,
now and forever.
AMEN!

The Lord's Prayer

The Peace of the Lord be always with you.
And also with you!

(The peace is shared)

We break this bread
In sharing it, we are one, each with the other.

Be - hold the Lamb of God, be - hold the La - mb of God. Who

takes a - way the sin, the - sin - of - the world.

(full music page 137)

Behold the Lamb of God,
Behold the Lamb of God,
Who takes away the sin,
The sin of the world.[49]

Holy things for holy people.
Only God is holy.

Distribution

As Jesus was sent into the world,
send us out.

Do not take us out of this world,
but protect us from the evil one.

When the world does not understand,
may the love that was in Jesus be in us.

We wait in the city, for the Spirit to come.,
Come, Holy Spirit, come!

We wait on the Saviour.
Come, Holy Spirit, come!

We wait on God.
Come, Holy Spirit, come!

49 Iona

take, bless, break, give

Pentecost

take, bless, break, give

Pentecost

Prayer

Holy Spirit,
breathing gently in the earth,
breathing rhythmically in the water,
breathing strong and firm in the wind,
breathing explosively in the fire,
breathing,
breathing,
breathing,
entering your people's dreams
with new tongues,
fresh voices of hope:

Come to us in our bewilderment:
teach us through the power of your Word.
Pray with us in our hearts,
bring peace,
bring joy.

We pray in the name of the One,
who promised the comforting Spirit at Pentecost
to disciples gathered together
then as now.
Amen!

Pentecost Eucharistic Prayer

(Bread and wine are brought to the table during the singing of a hymn)

God's Spirit is with us!
Thanks be to God!

Lift up your hearts!
We lift them to the Lord!

Let us give thanks to God!
It is just to give God thanks and praise!

We give You thanks
that at the beginning of time,
your Holy Spirit moved across the face of the waters,
separating night from day
sea from land
and breathing life into human flesh.
Embracing the new-born world with love.

Through your Holy Spirit,
the Prophets spoke the Word of judgement.
receiving your law,
challenging corruption,
announcing liberation from slavery,
prophecying exile and homecoming.
Giving birth to our dreams of freedom.

Through your Holy Spirit,
Jesus was anointed to preach Good News to the poor,
proclaim release to the captives,
restoration of sight to the blind,
liberation to all who are oppressed
and to proclaim the Jubilee,
in which we are all set free from our debts.
Through the crucifixion, resurrection and ascension,
the mighty have been put down from their thrones,
and the humble have been lifted up.

Through tongues of fire and mighty rushing wind,
your Holy Spirit came to the disciples gathered together
and it comes to us,

the same Spirit, the one Spirit,
which has protected and enlivened your people,
from generation to generation
and continent to continent.

Even now in the power of the Spirit,
we join with them in an everlasting hymn:

You are ho - ly, you are whole. You are al - ways ev - er more_ than we ev - er un - der - stand.

You are al - ways at hand_ Bless - ed are you com - ing near._ Bless - ed are you com - ing here

to your church in wine and bread, raised from soil, raised from dead._ You are ho ly -

- You are whole - ness You are pres - ent_ Let the cos - mos praise you Lord!

Hal - le - lu - ja Hal - le - lu - ja.

Hal - le - lu - ja,_ Hal - le - lu - ja our Lord

You are holy, you are whole,
You are always ever more
than we ever understand.
You are always at hand.
Blessed are you coming near,
Blessed are you coming here,
to your Church
in wine and bread,
raised from soil, raised from dead.
You are holy, you are wholeness,
you are present,
Let the cosmos praise you Lord,
Hallelujah, hallelujah,
Hallelujah, hallelujah our Lord![50]

50 Per Harling

You are holy,
and in the holiness of this moment,
we sense your Spirit,
moving from person to person.

Come in your power
and make us your people.
Come, Spirit, come!

May these gifts of bread and wine
be to us the body and blood of Jesus,
Who on the night of his arrest,
betrayal and torture
took bread,
blessed it,
broke it,
gave it to his disciples saying:
"Take, eat, this is my body,
which is given for you.
Do this in remembrance of me."

In the same way also
He took the cup,
after supper, saying:
"This is my blood of the New Covenant
poured out for many, for the forgiveness of sins.
As often as you drink it,
do it in remembrance of me."

As often as you eat this bread and drink the cup,
you proclaim the Lord's death, until he comes.

So in remembering you we proclaim our faith:
Christ has died!
Christ is risen!
Christ will come again!

In proclaiming our faith we enter into your sacrifice.
We offer our broken selves to you.
We offer a violated and violent world for your healing.

We pray for the power of the Spirit
to share the love of the Gospel,
with all who share this meal
and with the poor, the hungry, the mourning and the persecuted
throughout the world.

Pour down your Spirit upon this Assembly of your people,
may we be gathered into your kingdom,
and share this bread and this cup,
with all the saints,
forever praising you, the giver of all good things,
the source of our deepest dreams and warmest desire.

This we ask in the name of Jesus Christ,
our Risen and Ascended Lord,
through whom,
with whom,
in whom,
in the unity of the Holy Spirit,
all glory and honour are yours,
almighty God
now and forever.
AMEN!

The Lord's Prayer

The Peace of the Lord be always with you.
And also with you!

(The peace is shared)

We break this bread
In sharing it, we are one, each with the other.

Be - hold the Lamb of God, be - hold the La - mb of God. Who
takes a - way the sin, the - sin - of - the world.

(full music page 137)

Behold the Lamb of God,
Behold the Lamb of God,
Who takes away the sin,
The sin of the world.[51]

Holy things for holy people.
Only God is holy.

---

51 Iona

Distribution

During the distribution we sing,

(full music page 140)

**If you believe and I believe
and we together pray,
the Holy Spirit must come down
and set God's people free,
and set God's people free,
and set God's people free,
the Holy Spirit must come down,
and set God's people free.**[52]

Pentecostal Spirit,
stay with us,
as we go into the world,
give us courage,
strength,
love
wisdom.

**Praise God for the Spirit,
Praise God for our Spirit-filled lives.**

The powerless and downtrodden
are lifted up in the strength of God.
**Alleluia!
Alleluia!
Alleluia!**

Go in peace to love and serve the Lord!

**In the name of Christ
Amen!**

---

52 Zimbabwean traditional

Ordinary Time

take, bless, break, give

Ordinary Time

A simple Eucharist

(This prayer is particularly suitable where children are present. The celebrant should be free to extemporise – and relate the prayer to community issues)

We gather around the table,
to remember the last meal, which Jesus shared with his friends
before he died.

We also want to be together in a special way, close to each other
and close to Jesus.

What do we bring to the table?
(The bread and wine are explained and any other suitable things brought to the table, such as work from Christian education classes)

The Lord be with you!
And also with you!

Lift up your hearts!
We lift them to the Lord!

Let us give thanks to God!
It is right to give God thanks and praise!

We say thank you to God for the world,
for the sun,
and the stars,
for the moon,
and the planets,
Thank you God.

We say thank you to God for our lives,
for the air we breathe,
the food we eat,
the friends who are special to us,
the love we are given.
Thank you God

We say thank you to God,
because God protects us,
as God protected all who have lived before us.
Thank you God.

We say thank you to God,
for all the people in church today,
for all who love us,
for all who teach us God's way,
for all who show God's love to those in need.
Thank you God.

We say thank you to God,
for Jesus,
a friend of all who needed a friend,
a teacher of his disciples and followers,
a healer of the sick.
Thank you God.

We draw closer together
and closer to God -
God who is farther away from us
than the farthest star in the heavens,
and as close to us as our breathing.

You are holy, you are whole.
You are always ever more
than we ever understand.
You are always at hand.
Blessed are you coming near.
Blessed are you coming here
to your church in wine and bread,
raised from soil, raised from dead.
You are holy.
You are wholeness.
You are present.
Let the cosmos praise you Lord!
Hallelujah, Hallelujah, Hallelujah,
Hallelujah, our Lord[53]

And as we say thank you,
we also remember,
those who lived before us,
and everyone yet to be born.

We remember Jesus
Who on the night of his arrest,
betrayal and torture,
took bread,
blessed it,
broke it,
gave it to his disciples saying:
"Take, eat, this is my body,
which is given for you.
Do this in remembrance of me."

In the same way also
He took the cup,
after supper, saying:
"This is my blood of the New Covenant
poured out for many, for the forgiveness of sins.
As often as you drink it,
do it in remembrance of me."

As often as you eat this bread and drink the cup,
you proclaim the Lord's death, until he comes.

53 Per Harling - Sweden

We remember that Jesus died for us.
We celebrate that he is alive again.
We look forward to the coming of his Kingdom

We pray now for the Holy Spirit to come and to bless the bread and the wine to make them special for us:
the body and the blood of Jesus,
food for our spirits.

We offer this prayer in the name of Christ Jesus,
through whom,
with whom,
in whom,
in the unity of the Holy Spirit,
all glory and honour are yours,
almighty God,
now and forever.
AMEN!

The Lord's Prayer

The peace of the Lord be always with you.
And also with you!

(we share the peace)

We break this bread
In sharing it, we are one, each with the other.

Come, eat, for all is prepared.

we sing during the distribution:

Give me your hand,
Let us be forever,
On the life-long path,
Companions now together.
Give me your hand,
Sister wherever you travel,
Give me your hand,
Brother on narrow pathways.
Give me your hand,
Let us steadfast be in love,
And move towards where peace abides,
And move towards where peace abides.
Give us your hand, O God,
Guide us in our living,
Grant us your forgiving,
Give us your hand.[54]

We have shared this special time with Jesus and with each other.
We are ready to leave,
because we know that Jesus will stay with us.

**We go out together in the strength of God,
to serve God in the world,
through the love of our neighbour.
Amen, Amen, Amen.**

---

54 words Uwe Seidel music Fritz Baltrweit

take, bless, break, give

Festivals

take, bless, break, give

Festivals

Prayer

In the sweet caress,
In the tender touch,
In the softening tear,
In the lover's kiss,
And the closeness of sleep,
    Give glory to God.

In the fertile earth,
In the buried seed,
In the moistened dew,
In the fragile flowers,
And the harvested fruit,
    Give glory to God.

In the fiery sun,
In the round new moon,
In the distant stars,
In the certainty of day,
And the embrace of night,
    Give glory to God.

In the gladness of morning,
In the blessing of rising,
In the painfulness of birth,
In the vibrancy of life,
And the silence of death,
    Give glory to God.

Festival Eucharistic Prayer

The table is set with fruit, bread and wine.

God made a promise:
A feast for all to share.

**We are God's people,
tired of waiting,
despairing of believing.**

We are God's people,
hungry for love,
thirsty for justice.

**We are God's people,
dreaming of sharing,
hoping of believing.**

Lift up your hearts!
We lift them to God!

Let us give thanks to God!
It is right to give God thanks and praise!

This is the banquet God has prepared.
God's Word comes true in our hearing.

God's promise is kept
in creation's dawning day.

Within
the light, the night,
the stars, the moon,
the sun, the sky,
the sea, the sand
see - God's plenty:
**Taste and see,
our God is gracious.**

Within
the corn, the maize,
the rice, the fruit,
the milk, the fish,
the bread, the wine,
taste - God's plenty:

**Taste and see,
our God is gracious.**

God's promise is kept,
in creation's dying day.

Within
slaves leaving Egypt,
Promised Land arriving,
Babylon destroying,
exiles surviving,
see - God's faithfulness:
**Taste and see,
our God is gracious.**

Within,
prison's deathly chamber,
torture's silent witness
saint's defiant prayers
our beloved – the disappeared,
taste - God's faithfulness:
**Taste and see,
our God is gracious.**

God's promise is kept
in creation's fulfilling day.

Our
love victorious,
hatred conquered,
shrouds removed,
death defeated.
See - God keeps promise:
**Taste and see,
our God is gracious.**

Our
table set, bread, wine,
feast beginning,
people seated,
poor, maimed, lame, blind.
Taste - God keeps promise.
**Taste and see,
our God is gracious.**

This is the banquet God has prepared.
We join your company,
disciples of the Way,
in communion with our ancestors,
saints and martyrs,
even with the angels,
your messengers of peace.

We are in their presence
feasting at the same table.

Ho - - ly,   Ho - ly,   Ho - ly.

(To be sung in canon)

Holy, Holy, Holy.[55]

You are holy and blessed,
the one we waited for.
We remember your love,
with gratitude.
We remember
and we believe.

A shattered dream,
in garden lost.
A rainbow sign,
on flooded earth.
A prophet's dream,
of Saviour's birth.
We remember
and we believe.

Jesus, brother,
walking, talking,
giving, forgiving,
touching, loving,
wounded healer,
broken lover,
crucified friend,
earth's salvation.
We remember
and we believe.

55 source unknown

Tomb opened,
storm stilled,
voice of hope,
resurrection -
"Peace be still."
"I am with you -
now and for always.
always and for always."
**We remember
and we believe.**

Pentecostal alleluias,
Spirit-born, fire anointing,
healed divisions,
your people one.
**We remember
and we believe.**

Spirit come,
now, as then,
unite your people,
break our sadness
**ALLELUIA!
Amen!**

Spirit's power - come
to free us.
Spirit's power - come
to bread and wine
transformed to be
the body,
the blood
of Jesus.
**Spirit's power, come!
ALLELUIA!
Amen!**

Jesus on the night of his arrest,
betrayal and torture
took bread,
blessed it,
broke it,
gave it to his disciples saying:
"Take, eat, this is my body,
which is given for you.
Do this in remembrance of me."

In the same way also
He took the cup,
after supper, saying:
"This is my blood of the New Covenant
poured out for many, for the forgiveness of sins.
As often as you drink it,
do it in remembrance of me."

As often as you eat this bread and drink the cup,
you proclaim the Lord's death, until he comes.

We remember together the sacrifice of Jesus, on the cross.
We believe, together, in his resurrection and everlasting presence.
We remember and we believe:
My Lord and my God!

Your sacrifice has given us life.
Fill our hearts with love.

Your rising has given us hope.
Wipe the tears from our eyes.

Your sacrifice enables us to carry the cross.
May your life inspire our lives.

Our memorial is a thanksgiving.
Our outpouring of love to You.

Holy Spirit
binding us to Jesus,
pointing us toward God,
present in the sharing of bread and wine,
uniting us with all who have lived,
and all yet to be born.

Sacrifice of Jesus,
bequeathing us the Holy Spirit,
reconciling us to God.
calling us to be servants of the poor,
and humbling us before our neighbour.

God of time and space,
Father of our Lord Jesus Christ,
Source of the Holy Spirit,
make us one,

**committed to the liberation of time
and the freedom of space.
Make us one body
united in one love.**

Thus united we pray
for all people of faith,
for all who strive for justice,
for those Jesus called blessed:
the poor, the mourning, the hungry, the persecuted.

Together
with those who have died in your love,
those who pray with us for your Kingdom to come,
we look forward to the time of peace and justice
we know is yet to be,
promised by Jesus,
the source of this feast of joy,
in which we now share
**through whom,
with whom,
in whom,
in the unity of the Holy Spirit,
all glory and honour are yours,
almighty God,
now and forever.
AMEN!**

So let us pray
the prayer of the kingdom.

The Lord's Prayer

This is the Kingdom of peace.
This is the feast of life.

The peace of the Lord be always with you.
And also with you!

We share the peace

We are many,
And yet we all share in the one bread.

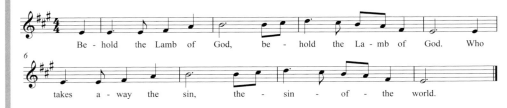

(full music page 137)

Behold the Lamb of God,
Behold the Lamb of God,
Who takes away the sin,
The sin of the world.

Holy things for holy people.
Only God is holy.

Distribution

Fed
No longer hungry.

Satisfied
No longer thirsty.

Equal
No longer strangers.

Friends
Travelling companions.

God's children
Jesus' disciples.

With food for the journey,
hope for the dawn,
with peace for our neighbour,
love for the world,
we go on our way
in peace.

God be with you!
God be with us all.
AMEN

Blessings

take, bless, break, give

Blessings

A blessing of creation

May the blessing of the rivers and hills be upon you;
the blessing of the sea and sky be upon you;
the blessing of picture, poetry and music be upon you;
the blessing of laughter and tears be upon you;
the blessing of tenderness and touch be upon you;
the blessing of wisdom and tranquillity be upon you;
the blessing of the Creator be upon you;
the blessing of the Saviour living among us, be upon you;
the blessing of the Spirit, stirring, demanding, transforming and
giving peace, rest with you.
Amen

A blessing of faith

The blessing of our ancestors, from generation to generation be upon us;
the blessing of the Word of God read from loving lips be upon us;
the blessing of the People of God, active and strong be upon us;
the blessing of water, shaped as a cross be upon us;
the blessing of bread and wine, passed from friend to friend be upon us;
the blessing of God, creating and redeeming be upon us;
the blessing of the Son, sharing our homelessness and exile be upon us;
the blessing of the Holy Spirit, lifting up the fallen, healing the sick, rescuing the fleeing,
strengthening the downtrodden and giving power to the oppressed by upon us all,
for evermore
Amen.

Music

take, bless, break, give

Israeli Mass

The Israeli Mass – Anthony Hampson
© McCrimmon Publishing Co. Ltd., 10-13 High Street,
Great Wakering, Southend-on-Sea, Essex SS30EQ

Alleluia

Alleluia – George Mxadana
© Panel on Worship Church of Scotland, 121 George Street, Edinburgh EH8 9QY

Gloria

Gloria
Jacques Berthier Taize Community © Ateliers et Presses de Taize,
Taize Communaute F-71250, France

Holy, Holy, Holy (Pablo Sosa)

Holy, Holy, Holy – Santo – composer of melody unknown
(as taught by Pablo Sosa)
Arrangement © Iona Community

Holy, Holy, Holy

Holy Holy Holy: Source unknown

Holy, Holy, Holy (S.C.Mxadana)

Holy, Holy, Holy – South Africa melody attributed to S.C. Molefe
(as taught by S.C.Mxadana) adapted by Vaughan Jones

Amen Siakudumesa

Amen Siakudumesa – South Africa melody attributed to S.C. Molefe
(as taught by S.C.Mxadana)

Behold the Lamb of God

Behold the Lamb of God
©   1995 WGRG, Iona Community, Glasgow G51 3UU

You are holy, you are whole

You are holy, you are whole – Per Harling Sweden (English translation
©   Per Harling (WCC?)

Christ be with me

Christ be with me
Attributed to St Patrick tr C.F.Alexander
Traditional Irish hymn melody arranged by Charles Villiers Stanford

Alleluia (Honduras)

Alleluia – Honduras
© 1995 WGRG, Iona Community, Glasgow G51 3UU Scotland

Give me your hand

Give me your hand, let us be for-ev-er on the life-long path.____ Com-pan-ions, now, to-
geth-er. Give me your hand, Sis-ter wher-ev-er we tra-vel. Give me your hand
Bro-ther on nar-row path-ways, Give_ me your hand, let us stead-fast be in love.____ And
move to-wards where peace a-bides and move to-wards where peace a - bides. Give us your hand O God,
Guide us in our liv - ing,__ Grant us your for - giv - ing.__ Give__ us your hand.

Give me your hand
All rights by © Dagmar Kamenzky, Music verlag, Hamburg, Germany
English words Irmgard Kindt-Siegwalt

Alleluia, the Lord is risen

Alleluia, the Lord is risen: source unknown

If you believe

If you believe Words and music Zimbabwean traditional (adapted from an English source) as taught by Tarasai. From Sent By the Lord – Songs of the World Church Wild Goose Publications Iona

Acknowledgments

Acknowledgments

With gratitude to the Pastors, Elders and worshipping community of Bethnal Green Meeting House.

To Becky Dudley for her persistence in wanting these prayers to reach a wider audience.

Bethnal Green Meeting House, now a United Reformed Church can trace its history to 1547, when villagers from the hamlets of Bethnal Green and Old Ford met in a Puritan Preaching Place. In 1662, the congregation refused to assent to the use of a Book of Common Prayer and formed an independent meeting place. With the industrial revolution, the Church found itself in the heart of the poorest corner of Britain and still does today. It was bombed during the Second World War and is situated but 100 yards from the location of the greatest civilian disaster of that war. Today, the worshipping community continues the radical tradition of independent worship.

The church building is shared with an African Pentecostal church, a Bengali supplementary mother-tongue school and Praxis a voluntary organisation, working in a practical way for the human rights of refugees, asylum seekers and migrant workers.

Cover: Photographs by Carlos Reyes-Manzo/Andes Press Agency. Used by permission.

Israeli Mass
© McCrimmon Publishing Co. Ltd. Used with permission.

Gloria
music: Jacques Berthier (1923 –1994)
© Ateliers et Presses de Taizé, 71250 Taizé-Community, France.

Alleluia
From *Come all you people* (Wild Goose Publications, 1995)
words: Trad. Liturgical Music: From Honduras, source unknown
Arrangement © 1995 WGRG, Iona Community, Glasgow G2 3DH.

Behold the lamb of God
From *Come all you people* (Wild Goose Publications, 1995)
Words: Jn 1.29 Music by John L Bell
© 1995 WGRG, Iona Community, Glasgow, G2 3DH

Santo
From *Many and great* (Wild Goose Publications, 1990)
words: variation on trad. Liturgical text.
Music: Argentina, source unknown
Arrangement: John L Bell
© 1990 WGRG, Iona Community, Glasgow G2 3DH

If you believe and I believe
From *Sent by the Lord* (Wild Goose Publications, 1991)
words: Trad. Based on Matthew 18:19
Music: Zimbabwean variant of an English folk melody.
Arrangement: John L Bell
© 1991 WGRG, Iona Community, Glasgow G2 3DH

Extracts from **Common Worship: Services and Prayers for the Church of England**: Psalms 55, 59, 64, 88 and 130
Copyright © The Archbishops' Council 2000.
Used by permission.

Give to me your hand by Dagmar Kamenzky,
English words by Irmgard Kindt-siegwalt
and
You are holy, you are whole
by Per Harling

from **In Spirit and in Truth** © 1991 World Council of Churches, 150 route de Ferney, 1211 Geneva 2, Switzerland.
Permission sought.